# SMALL TALK

## A Book of Short Poems

*Selected by Lee Bennett Hopkins*

*Illustrated by Susan Gaber*

*Harcourt Brace & Company*

*San Diego   New York   London*

Compilation copyright © 1995 by Lee Bennett Hopkins
Illustrations copyright © 1995 by Susan Gaber

Requests for permission to make copies
of any part of the work should be mailed to:
Permissions Department, Harcourt Brace & Company,
6277 Sea Harbor Drive, Orlando, Florida 32887-6777.

Permission acknowledgments appear on page 47,
which constitutes a continuation of the copyright page.

Library of Congress Cataloging-in-Publication Data
Small talk: a book of short poems / selected
by Lee Bennett Hopkins; illustrated by Susan Gaber.
p. cm.
Summary: A collection of short poems by such writers
as Richard Wilbur, Langston Hughes, and X. J. Kennedy.
ISBN 0-15-276577-8
1. Children's poetry, American. [1. American poetry —
Collections.] I. Hopkins, Lee Bennett. II. Gaber, Susan, ill.
PS586.3.S76    1995
811.008'09282 — dc20        94-7601

First edition        A B C D E

Printed in Singapore

The illustrations in this book were done in watercolor
and colored pencil on Strathmore Bristol board.
The display type was set in Simoncini Garamond, and the text type was
set in Stempel Garamond by Thompson Type, San Diego, California.
Color separations by Bright Arts, Ltd., Singapore
Printed and bound by Tien Wah Press, Singapore
This book was printed with soya-based inks on Leykam recycled
paper, which contains more than 20 percent postconsumer waste
and has a total recycled content of at least 50 percent.
Production supervision by Warren Wallerstein and David Hough
Designed by Camilla Filancia

# CONTENTS

## S S S H

*Betsy Hearne*

Spring whispers secret

rain to the listening trees

till they shout loud green.

## ROBIN

*J. Patrick Lewis*

Suddenly Spring wings

into the backyard, ready

to play tug-of-worm.

# S P R I N G

*Prince Redcloud*

How pleasing—

not

to be

freezing.

# RAIN

*Emanuel di Pasquale*

Like a drummer's brush,

the rain hushes the surface of tin porches.

# LET'S COUNT THE RAINDROPS
*Alan Benjamin*

Let's count the raindrops

as they pour:

one million, two million,

three million, four.

# CATERPILLAR

*Tony Johnston*

Caterpillar. Bulgy. Brown.

Creeping up the rose.

Soon he will be beautiful

In his party clothes.

# CATERPILLAR'S LULLABY
### *Jane Yolen*

Your sleep will be
a lifetime
and all your dreams
rainbows.
Close your eyes
and spin yourself
a fairytale:
Sleeping Ugly,
Waking Beauty.

# WHAT ARE HEAVY?

*Christina G. Rossetti*

What are heavy? Sea-sand and sorrow.

What are brief? Today and tomorrow.

What are frail? Spring blossoms and youth.

What are deep? The ocean and truth.

## LIFE

*Lee Bennett Hopkins*

Newborn kittens
stumbled slowly
toward their mother.

Snuggling into
her
tired-warm belly

they
readied for
their
first
Wednesday morning
banquet.

# A SNAIL'S NEEDS
# ARE VERY SMALL
*Patricia Hubbell*

Sea-foam,
wet stone,
shell home.

These three
please me
mightily.

## IN THE SAND

*Myra Cohn Livingston*

In the sand
A castle grows
    (ramps and towers, turrets, bowers, trees and flowers)
    and for hours
    kings and knights march through the land

    in between my toes.

# ROCKS

*Florence Parry Heide*

Big rocks into pebbles,

pebbles into sand.

I really hold a million million rocks here in my hand.

# RELEASE

### *A. R. Ammons*

After a long
muggy
hanging
day
the raindrops
started so
sparse
the bumblebee flew
between
them home.

21

## SUMMER COOLER
*X. J. Kennedy*

In the summer young Angus McQuade

Carries off to his castle of shade

    Two cool soothing pillows,

    *The Wind in the Willows*,

And an ocean of iced lemonade.

# LITTLE JUMPING JOAN
*Mother Goose*

Here am I, Little Jumping Joan,

When nobody's with me

I'm always alone.

# HOPE

*Langston Hughes*

Sometimes when I'm lonely,

Don't know why,

Keep thinkin' I won't be lonely

By and by.

## OPPOSITES

*Richard Wilbur*

What is the opposite of *two*?

*A lonely me, a lonely you.*

# BULLETIN

*A. R. Ammons*

I mentioned trimming

the bushes and

the squirrels cleared

their nuts out of there

27

# THE CITY

*David Ignatow*

If flowers want to grow

right out of concrete sidewalk cracks

I'm going to bend down to smell them

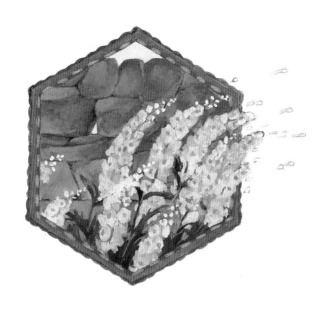

## C H A N G E

*Lee Bennett Hopkins*

When the first petals blow
the timeless stone wall
knows the reason:

Summer has grown old
ebbing toward
a sleep-time
season.

# BALLOONING SPIDERS
*Rebecca Kai Dotlich*

On a thin silver string

wee spiderlings

sweep over the sea.

# GROWING UP
## *Aileen Fisher*

When I grow up

(as everyone does)

what will become

of the Me I was?

# THE SPAN OF LIFE

*Robert Frost*

The old dog barks backward without getting up.

I can remember when he was a pup.

# FOSSIL FINDS
### *Rebecca Kai Dotlich*

No skin,
no scale,
no ancient moan —
his legacy is strictly

BONE.

# F O G

*J. Patrick Lewis*

The
bone-
deep
chill
of
early
fall
when
night
slips
in-
to
her
white
silk
shawl

# TODAY
### *Lillian M. Fisher*

Today the bay

is lonely —

Only one small ship

comes home.

# EVENING
*Sara Teasdale*

Blue dust of evening over my city,

Over the ocean of roofs and the tall towers

Where the window-lights, myriads and myriads,

Bloom from the walls like climbing flowers.

# FOGHORNS

*Lilian Moore*

The foghorns moaned

    in the bay last night

so sad

so deep

I thought I heard the city

    crying in its sleep.

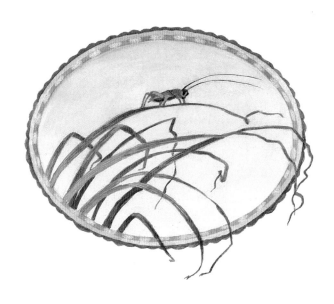

# S P L I N T E R

## *Carl Sandburg*

The voice of the last cricket

across the first frost

is one kind of good-by.

It is so thin a splinter of singing.

# WINTER DAY
### *Aileen Fisher*

You make a snowman

and put a necktie on it.

I'll make a snow*ma'am*

and have her wear a bonnet.

# WET SOCKS
## *James Hayford*

Nothing I own

Is sure to improve with time

Like these wet socks

On the radiator

That I'll put on

Dry and warm

Later.

# SILENCE

*Eve Merriam*

Quiet,
so quiet
without a sound

floating,
falling
to the ground

snowflake feathers
from snow-white birds

snow is a poem
without any words.

# A POEM SO SPUN

*Victoria Forrester*

Paper windmills,
softly blow;
let them turn,
let them go.
A poem so spun
may bring delight
and words to keep
against the night.

# Permission Acknowledgments

Every effort has been made to trace the ownership of all copyrighted material and to secure permissions to reprint these selections. In the event of any question arising as to the use of any material, the editor and the publisher, while expressing regret for any inadvertent error, will make the necessary correction in future printings. Thanks are due to the following for permission to reprint the material listed below:

BOA Editions Limited for "Rain" from *Genesis* by Emanuel di Pasquale, copyright © 1989 by Emanuel di Pasquale. Reprinted with the permission of BOA Editions Limited, 92 Park Avenue, Brockport, NY 14420.

Curtis Brown Ltd. for "Life" by Lee Bennett Hopkins, copyright © 1981 by Lee Bennett Hopkins; "Change" by Lee Bennett Hopkins, copyright © 1995 by Lee Bennett Hopkins; "Caterpillar's Lullaby" from *Dragon Night* by Jane Yolen, copyright © 1980 by Jane Yolen. All reprinted by permission of Curtis Brown Ltd.

Rebecca Kai Dotlich for "Ballooning Spiders" and "Fossil Finds." Used by permission of the author, who controls all rights.

Aileen Fisher for "Winter Day." Used by permission of the author, who controls all rights.

Lillian M. Fisher for "Today." Used by permission of the author, who controls all rights.

Harcourt Brace & Company for "Splinter" from *Good Morning, America* by Carl Sandburg, copyright 1928 and renewed 1956 by Carl Sandburg; poem "12" from *Opposites: Poems and Drawings* by Richard Wilbur, copyright © 1973 by Richard Wilbur. Both reprinted by permission of Harcourt Brace & Company.

HarperCollins Publishers for "Growing Up" from *Always Wondering* by Aileen Fisher, copyright © 1991 by Aileen Fisher. Reprinted by permission of HarperCollins Publishers.

Florence Parry Heide for "Rocks." Used by permission of the author, who controls all rights.

Henry Holt & Company, Inc., for "The Span of Life" from *The Poetry of Robert Frost*, edited by Edward Connery Lathem, copyright 1936 by Robert Frost, copyright © 1964 by Leslie Frost Ballantine, copyright © 1969 by Henry Holt & Company, Inc. Reprinted by permission of Henry Holt & Company, Inc.

Tony Johnston for "Caterpillar." Used by permission of the author, who controls all rights.

Alfred A. Knopf, Inc., for "Hope" from *Selected Poems* by Langston Hughes, copyright 1942 by Alfred A. Knopf, Inc., and renewed 1970 by Arna Bontemps and George Houston Bass. Reprinted by permission of the publisher.

Macmillan Publishing Company for "A Poem So Spun" from *Words to Keep Against the Night* by Victoria Forrester, copyright © 1983 by Victoria Forrester. Reprinted with permission of Atheneum Publishers, an imprint of Macmillan Publishing Company; "Sssh" from *Polaroid*